EXIT THROUGH THE GIFT SHOP

**Written By
Jennifer Rankins
In collaboration with
Melvin Rankins**

John 3:16 is the Biblical definition of Love. It tells us: "For God so loved the world that He gave His only begotten son, and whosoever believeth in Him, shall not parish but have ever lasting life."

This little book is dedicated to the Fruit of the Spirit in every Believer. If you're not sure you have any one of these nine Fruit of the Spirit, you can always Exit through the Gift Shop and pick some up along the way. Remember, every gift from God is FREE.

Text copyright © 2018 by Melvin and Jennifer Rankins
All rights reserved.

First Edition

Published by Create Space Publishing Company

ISBN: 9781985341401

Cover Design by Create Space Publishing and its Affiliates
Author photograph taken by Kinja Walton

INTRODUCTION

When the apostle Paul penned the nine qualities in Galatians we call the **"Fruit of the Spirit,"** he neatly divided them into three general groups, though some overlapping of application occurs between them. The **first group**—love, joy and peace—portrays a Christian's mind in its most general form, that deal with the soul's wellbeing, with special emphasis on his relationship with God. The **second group**, beginning with patience ("longsuffering" in the KJV), kindness, and goodness, contains social virtues relating to our thoughts and actions towards our fellow man and our attitude during trials and tribulations. And the **third group** beginning with faithfulness, gentleness, and self-control deals with those attributes that provide principles for the believer's proper conduct.

*"Now the deeds of the flesh are evident, which are: immorality, impurity, sensuality, idolatry, sorcery, enmities, strife, jealousy, outbursts of anger, disputes, dissensions, factions, envying, drunkenness, carousing, and things like these, of which I forewarn you, just as I have forewarned you, that those who practice such things **will not inherit the kingdom of God**.*

The Fruit of the Spirit is a biblical term that sums up nine attributes of a person or community living in accord with the Holy Spirit according to Galatians: "But the Fruit of the Spirit is love, joy, peace, patience, kindness, goodness, faithfulness, gentleness, and self-control." The fruit is contrasted with the works of the flesh which immediately precede it in the chapter.

If we live by the Spirit, let us also walk by the Spirit. Let us not become boastful, challenging one another, envying one another."

So, what exactly will you will find inside the Gift Shop?

Well, I'm glad you asked that question.

In order to understand the Fruit of the Spirit, we must first understand who the Spirit is, what He does and how He helps us live our lives pleasing to God. Notice there is no "s" on the end of Fruit, but a singular word. That's because all of the Fruit of the Spirit is combined into one and is freely given to every believer.

So, where exactly will you find the Fruit of the Spirit? We suggest before you leave church next Sunday, don't leave without Exiting through the Gift Shop.

INSIDE THIS GIFT SHOP YOU WILL FIND PLENTY OF THESE:

HOW TO GROW THE PERFECT GARDEN

PLANT THREE ROWS OF PEAS:
1. PEACE OF MIND
2. PEACE OF HEART
3. PEACE OF SOUL

PLANT FOUR ROWS OF SQUASH:
1. SQUASH OUT GOSSIP
2. SQUASH INDIFFERENCE
3. SQUASH SELFISHNESS
4. SQUASH GRUMBLING

PLANT FOUR ROWS OF LETTUCE:
1. LETTUCE BE FAITHFUL
2. LETTUCE BE KIND
3. LETTUCE BE PATIENT
4. LETTUCE LOVE ONE ANOTHER

NO GARDEN SHOULD BE COMPLETE WITHOUT TURNIPS:
1. TURNIP FOR SERVICES
2. TURNIP FOR WORSHIP
3. TURNIP TO HELP ONE ANOTHER

TO CONCLUDE OUR GARDEN, WE MUST HAVE THYME:
1. TIME FOR GOD
2. TIME FOR FAMILY
3. TIME FOR FRIENDS
4. TIME FOR EACH OTHER

CONTINUE CULTIVATING YOUR GARDEN:

WATER FREELY WITH PATIENCE AND CULTIVATE WITH LOVE. IF YOU DO THIS, THERE WILL BE MUCH FRUIT TO PICK FROM IN YOUR GARDEN BECAUSE YOU REAP WHAT YOU SOW.

PART ONE

*This first group—**love, joy and peace**—portrays a Christian's mind in its most general form, with special emphasis on our relationship with God.*

CHAPTER 1
FIRST, GRAB A BASKET FULL OF
LOVE

Galatians 5: 22-23
*(But the fruit of the Spirit is **LOVE**, joy, peace, patience, kindness, goodness, faithfulness, gentleness, self-control; against such things there is no law.)*

This chapter about love is the longest of the nine Fruit of the Spirit description and attributes following. Why? Because in I Corinthians 13:13 says, *"Love is patient and kind, Love is not jealous, pain, conceited, anger, prideful or boastful, it is not arrogant, selfish, irritable or rude.* **Love does not keep a record of wrongs**. *Love is not happy with evil, but is happy with the truth, love never gives up, and its faith, hope and patience never fail. It always Protects, always Trusts, always Hopes, always Perseveres. But the greatest of these is love."*

"Love is patient, love is kind it does not envy or jealous, it does not boast, it is not proud. Love is not rude, it is not self-seeking or demands its own way, and it keeps no record of wrongs. Love does not delight or rejoice in evil but rejoices with the truth. Love always trusts and never gives up, it always hopes and never loses faith, always perseveres through every circumstance, love never ends."
I Corinthians 13: 1-13

<u>**So, what is Love?**</u>

The Greek definition for LOVE: agape, charity, affection, or benevolence. Love is the emotion of strong affection and personal attachments.

The word love can refer to a variety of different feelings, states, and attitudes, ranging from generic pleasure ("I loved that meal") to intense interpersonal attraction ("I love my partner"). "Love" can also refer specifically to the passionate desire and intimacy of romantic love also known as the sexual love of Eros – or to the emotional closeness of familial love, to the platonic love that defines friendship to the profound devotion of religious love. This diversity of uses and meanings, combined with the complexity of the feelings involved, makes love unusually difficult to consistently define, even compared to other emotional states.

In philosophical context, love is a virtue representing all of human kindness, compassion, and affection. In some religious contexts, love is not just a virtue, but the basis for all being, "God is love." Love may also be described as actions towards oneself based on compassion, or as actions towards others based on affection.

Love in its various forms acts as a major facilitator of interpersonal relationships and, owing to its central psychological importance, is one of the most common themes in the creative arts.

What does I-Corinthians 13: 4-7 say about Love?

Love never gives up.
Love cares more for others than for self.
Love doesn't want what it doesn't have.
Love doesn't strut,
Doesn't have a swelled head,
Doesn't force itself on others,
Isn't always "me first,"
Doesn't fly off the handle,

Doesn't keep score of the sins of others,
Doesn't revel when others grovel,
Takes pleasure in the flowering of truth,
Puts up with anything,
Trusts God always,
Always looks for the best,
Never looks back,
But keeps going to the end.

Vs. 9-10 Love never dies. Vs. 13 But for right now, until that completeness, we have three things to do to lead us toward that consummation or will last forever: Trust or have faith steadily in God, hope unswervingly, and love extravagantly. And the best of these three is LOVE.

The word "love" can have a variety of related but distinct meanings in different contexts. Often, other languages use multiple words to express some of the different concepts that English relies mainly on "love" to encapsulate the truest meaning of love, thus making it difficult to establish any one universal definition.

Although the nature or essence of love is a subject of frequent debate, different aspects of the word can be clarified by determining what love isn't. As a general expression of positive sentiment (a stronger form of like), love is commonly contrasted with hate (or neutral apathy); as a less sexual and more emotionally intimate form of romantic attachment, love is commonly contrasted with lust; and as an interpersonal relationship with romantic overtones, love is sometimes contrasted with friendship, although the word is often applied to close friendships.

The word love can mean many different things in the English language. It can refer to a mother's love for her child, love of country, romantic love, friendship, or God's love towards mankind. The original manuscripts of the New Testament of the Bible were written in the Greek language so we will take a look at the actual words used in the original manuscripts.

We will explore the following Greek words: *Agape, Phileas, and Eros Love*

AGAPE LOVE – WHAT IS IT?

Agape Love doesn't mean to love somebody because they're worthy. Agape makes them worthy by the strength and power of its love. Agape doesn't love somebody because they're beautiful. Agape loves in such a way that it makes them beautiful.

Often times, when we need love and grace the most is when we deserve it the least. Thank God that His love isn't determined by our worthiness, but by His choice.

Agape is defined as the love that God has for his Son and toward mankind. John 3:16 "For God so loved (agape) the world that He gave his one and only Son, that whoever believes in Him shall not perish but have everlasting life." Notice the first part of this verse says, "God so loved (**Agape**)... He gave." Agape love gives, and is the deep and constant love of a perfect being (God) towards an unworthy object (mankind).

Ephesians 2:4 - 5 "*But because of his great love (agape) for us, God, who is rich in mercy, made us alive with Christ even when we were dead in transgressions - it is by grace you have been saved.*"

Romans 5:8 "But God demonstrates his own love (agape) for us in this: While we were still sinners, Christ died for us." We were unworthy objects, we were sinners. Christ died for us." We were unworthy objects, we were sinners.

Agape love comes only from God

Does not always run with natural inclinations
Gives unselfishly
Takes action and is visible (you can see it in action)
Ready to serve
Does what is best
Not drawn out by Excellency
Deliberate choice without cause

I John 4:7 *"Dear friends, let us love (agape) one another, for love (agape) comes from God. Everyone who loves (agape) has been born of God and knows God. Agape love is love that only comes from God."*

I John 4:9-10 – This is how God showed his love (agape) among us: He sent his one and only Son into the world that we might live through him. This is love (agape): not that we loved (agape) God but that he loved (agape) us and sent his Son as an atoning sacrifice for our sins.

As you can see from this verse, agape love does not always run with natural inclinations nor does it spend itself only upon those for whom some affinity is discovered. Agape love gives unselfishly and takes action in a visible way. As sinners, we deserved the death that Jesus took upon himself on the cross. We were unworthy of the love that God demonstrated toward us when he allowed his only Son to die on the cross for us.

Agape love is why Jesus took action to choose to die on the cross for our sins in such a visible and humiliating way before all creation. Agape love truly does take action in a visible and if necessary humiliating way. Agape love is God doing what is best for mankind and not necessarily what man desires. Agape love is not drawn out by Excellency in its objects. It is an exercise of the divine will in deliberate choice, made without assignable cause.

Agape Love:
Comes only from God
Does not always run with natural inclinations
Gives unselfishly
Takes action and is visible (you can see it in action)
Ready to serve
Does what is best
Not drawn out by Excellency
Deliberate choice without cause

When we love one another with an agape type love, the Spirit of God can work through us in the lives of other people that need to see the love of Jesus.

Phileo Love

In contrast, philia love is defined as to be a friend to, indicating feelings, warm affection. As we study love, we begin to understand that phileo is the love that can come easily because of like interests, commonalities. Sometimes we meet people who we naturally like. They are easy to get along with, you may share the same ideas, they're likable and enjoyable to be around so you feel comfortable and have good feelings being around them. Many times, you develop a warm affection toward them and enjoy their company. You become friends. This is Phileo or brotherly love.

Phileo is never used in a command to men to love (phileo) God. Some want to say that God has only agape love but this isn't true. Take a look at the following verses.

John 3:35 *"The Father loves **(agape)** the Son and has placed everything in his hands, whoever believes in the Son has eternal life, but whoever rejects the Son will not see life, for God's wrath remains on him."*

John 5:20 "*For the Father loves **(phileo)** the Son and shows him all he does. Yes, to your amazement he will show him even greater things than these.*"

Phileas Love -Vs- Agape Love:

There Jesus had fish cooking on burning coals and invited them saying "Come and have breakfast." When they had finished breakfast, the following dialogue took place and is recorded in John 21:15-17: "*When they had finished eating, Jesus said to Simon Peter, "Simon son of John, do you truly love me more than these?"*

"*Yes, Lord*, "he said, "*you know that I love you.*" Jesus said, "*Feed my lambs.*" Again, Jesus said, "*Simon son of John, do you truly AGAPE me?*" He answered, "*Yes, Lord, you know that I love you.*" Jesus said "*Take care of my sheep.*" The third time he said to him, "*Simon son of John, do you AGAPE me?*" Peter was hurt because Jesus asked him the third time, "*Do you AGAPE me?*" He said, "*Lord, you know all things, you know that I love you.*" Jesus said, "*Feed my sheep.*"

Loving one another (agape love) is one of the greatest outward expressions of our devotion to God. Jesus demonstrated agape love towards Peter even though Peter had failed so many times as evidenced in the verses listed above. Jesus was entrusting to Peter to be a leader in the Church when he said to Peter "Feed my sheep."

A Pharisee asked Jesus "*Which is the greatest commandment?*" Let's look at Mathew 22:37-40 - Jesus replied "*Love the Lord your God with all your heart and with all your soul and with your entire mind. This is the first and greatest commandment. And the second is like it. Love your neighbor as yourself. All the law and the Prophets hang on these two commandments.*" Loving one another with an Agape type love shows our love for God and to God.

John 14:15 - "If you love (agape) me, you will obey what I command." John 15:12 - "My command is this: Love (agape) each other as I have loved (agape) you." I John 4:20 & 21 - If anyone says, "I love God," yet hates his brother, he is a liar. For anyone who does not love his brother, whom he has seen, cannot love God, whom he has not seen. And he has given us this command: Whoever loves God must also love his brother.

Eros Love

The **word Eros**, from which we get the English word *Erotic*, was the word often used to express sexual love or the feelings of arousal that are shared between people who are physically attracted to one another. The word was also used as the name of the Greek god of love, Eros (the Romans called him "Cupid"). By New Testament times, this word had become so debased by the culture that it is not used even once in the entire New Testament.

In the classical world, erotic love was generally referred to as a kind of madness or *theia mania* ("madness from the gods"). This love passion was described through an elaborate metaphoric and mythological schema involving "love's arrows" or "love darts", the source of which was often the personified figure of Eros (or his Latin counterpart, Cupid), or another deity (such as rumor). At times the source of the arrows was said to be the image of the beautiful love object itself. If these arrows were to arrive at the lover's eyes, they would then travel to and 'pierce' or 'wound' his or her heart and overwhelm him/her with desire and longing (lovesickness). The image of the "arrow's wound" was sometimes used to create oxymoron's and rhetorical antithesis concerning its pleasure and pain.

What does Philippians 1: 9-11 say about Love:

Paul and Timothy, both were committed servants of Christ Jesus. Paul wrote this letter (Philippians) to all the followers of Jesus in Philippi, pastors and ministers included, to admonish them of their continued work in the ministry.

"So, this is my prayer: that your love will flourish and that you will not only love much but well. Learn to love appropriately. You need to use your head and test your feelings so that your love is sincere and intelligent, not sentimental gush. Live a lover's life, circumspect and exemplary, a life Jesus will be proud of: bountiful in fruits from the soul, making Jesus Christ attractive to all, getting everyone involved in the glory and praise of God."

In Summary

Love is eternal as Love is the Master Key that opens the gate of happiness and it is a home deep down your heart as Love gives without taking and shares completely. Love brightens the day and nights of so many lives. Love sees no color, age, weight, gender, religion, political affiliation, or looks; it only sees what is in your heart, with Love as one door closes, another opens! Love is patient and kind, Love is not jealous, pain, conceited, anger, prideful or boastful, it is not arrogant, selfish, irritable or rude. **Love does not keep a record of wrongs.** Love is not happy with evil, but is happy with the truth, love never gives up, and its faith, hope and patience never fail. It always Protects, always Trusts, always Hopes, always Perseveres. But the greatest of these is love.

So, remember to take up a huge basket filled with love, and give the love that is inside you to Uplift, Inspire, Encourage & Support one another!

CHAPTER 2
THROW IN BUSSHELS OF
JOY

Galatians 5: 22-23
(But the fruit of the Spirit is love, JOY, peace, patience, kindness, goodness, faithfulness, gentleness, self-control; against such things there is no law.)

Joy Defined

The Greek definition for JOY is Chara, which means cheerfulness, calm, delight, and exceedingly glad.

Webster's New World Dictionary defines JOY as synonymous with "happy," "glad," and "cheerful." A thesaurus relates it to "exultation," "rapture," "satisfaction" and "pleasure." Webster's specifically defines it as "a very glad feeling; happiness; great pleasure; delight." It also refers to the source and cause of delight.

These definitions only define the expression of the wonderful emotion. They fail to consider the causes of joy, the circumstances in which it is expressed or its longevity. In these areas, the Bible presents a much more complex virtue than these definitions indicate.

Short-Lived Joy

A Christian's joy can be just as short-lived as anyone else in the world if we are seeking it for itself as the world does. Biblical joy is a fruit, a byproduct, an additional blessing, not the end in itself. It flows into and grows within the person whose life is focused merely on being "joyful." The lives of those in this world who are so zealously chasing after it proves this point. If they are still chasing it, they must not yet have it. God's Word also substantiates this. In this regard, we need to be aware that our pursuit of joy that it does not obscure the more important elements in our life.

Psalm 81 is a festival psalm, and verses 1-4: *"Sing aloud to God our strength; make a joyful shout (or noise) unto the God of Jacob. Raise a song and strike the timbral, the pleasant harp with the lute. Blow the trumpet at the time of the New Moon, at the full moon, on our solemn feast day. For this is a statute for Israel, a law of the God of Jacob."*

Does anyone on earth not want to live confidently and joyfully? Undoubtedly, out of six billion people, a few are so soured on life they would rather be dead, a thought they express in their downcast, grumbling and sometimes even snarling demeanor. However, they must be a trifling number in contrast to those who sincerely desire to possess joy in overflowing abundance.

Biblical joy is inseparable from our relationship with God and springs from our knowledge and understanding of the purpose of life, and the hope of living with God for eternity when there will be joy evermore. If God is actually present in our lives, the joy He experiences can begin in us. Joy is the sign that life has found its purpose, its reason for being! This, too, is a revelation of God, for no one can come to Him and find the purpose of life unless He, by the Holy Spirit, calls him and reveals it.

Quite a number of verses show that the JOY of God arises from sources other than those sought by the world. Notice how the early believers found joy:

Finding Joy in the Journey of Relationships:

JOY is a kind of relationship glue. It gives us intrinsic motivation to pursue intimacy and oneness in marriage. Bill Bright says it this way: "As long as you're going to be married the rest of your life, you might as well enjoy it." In other words, marriage is supposed to be a source of joy.

And joy is God's plan for our marriage. Throughout the Bible, marriage is used as a picture of joy that God feels for his people. For instance, the prophet Isaiah tells us, "As a bridegroom rejoices over his bride, so God will rejoice over you" (Isaiah 62:5).

JOY does two things for our marriages: 1) It causes us to remember the good. When something wonderful or fun or funny happens, as we go through the years together, we often look back on that experience and have almost as much joy reliving it. 2) Joy also causes us to live in the present. That's a place far too few of us live often enough. For just a moment when we're experiencing joy, thoughts of what's to come and all the things we need to do vanish. That's a great gift to give our marriages.

How does joy come in marriages? It comes by making a pledge to pursue oneness in marriage. Through commitment and fidelity. Commitment isn't just about avoiding divorce. The kind of commitment God calls His people to make isn't just to say, "I'll try to get to the end of my life without having a sexual relationship with somebody other than my spouse." No, it's an everyday commitment, every hour, every week and month and year to pursue to be greater in oneness, and also a commitment to pursue joy.

Being Positive in a Negative World

Complaining kills joy. It makes you unhappy. It makes everyone around you unhappy too. How many of you like to be around complainers? The problem is that once we start complaining it is hard to stop. Complaining can become a habit, and to tell you the truth – it is a bad habit. We can find something to complain about all the time. If it is raining, of course we can complain about that. But we could also rejoice that the ground is being refreshed and watered. If it is sunny we could complain about that saying, "Oh no, I will probably get sun-burned."

We are somewhat conditioned by our society to complain. Look at the headlines in your newspapers and on television. I would say that most of what you see is bad news. We are bombarded continuously with what's wrong with everything. By our own nature and by our conditioning we tend to develop the habit of complaining. But that is not how the Bible tells us to respond in a negative world. Look at Philippians chapter two:

"Do all things without complaining and disputing, that you may become blameless and harmless, children of God without fault in the midst of a crooked and perverse generation, among whom you shine as lights in the world, holding fast the word of life, so that I may rejoice in the day of Christ that I have not run in vain or labored in vain." Philippians 2:14-16 (NKJV)

The Bible tells us that Christians are to be different than the rest of the world. I like the way the Message Bible states these verses:

"Do everything readily and cheerfully—no bickering, no second-guessing allowed! Go out into the world uncorrupted, a breath of fresh air in this squalid and polluted society. Provide people with a glimpse of good living and of the living God. Carry the light-giving Message into the night so I'll have good cause to be proud of you on the day that Christ returns. You'll be living proof that I didn't go to all this work for nothing." Philippians 2:14-16 (MSG)

So, take up as many bushels of Joy as you cart can hold, it's a sign that your life has found its purpose.

CHAPTER 3
GRAB A CART FULL OF
PEACE

Galatians 5: 22-23
(But the fruit of the Spirit is love, joy, **PEACE**, *patience, kindness, goodness, faithfulness, gentleness, self-control; against such things there is no law.)*

What exactly is Peace?

The Greek definition for Peace is Eirene, which means quietness, calm, rest, or reset again.

There's a lot of Peace going around. Let's take a look at some:
Peacekeepers
Peace Corps
Peace Signs
Peace Lilly
Justice of the Peace

As we mentioned early, a garden can have several rows of peas planted:
1. PEACE OF MIND
2. PEACE OF HEART
3. PEACE OF SOUL
4. PEACE IN THE MIDST OF THE STORM

But, what does it mean to have peace?

Peacefulness is an inner sense of calm - it comes from becoming still – in order to reflect and meditate on our inner wisdom and receive answers. A peaceful heart is one that is free from worry and trouble. It's becoming quiet so we can look at things more clearly and understand them better, thus come up with creative solutions. It is learning to live in the present.

Peace comes from living in the moment and looking for the good in others. Peacefulness comes from facing our fears and letting them go - trusting that things will turn out all right. Peacefulness is also a way of approaching conflict with others so no one is made wrong, everyone wins because we work to find a peaceful solution.

So, what does the Bible say peace is?
What exactly is peace?
What is your idea of being at peace?

Is it a place – such as being at home alone after the kids have gone to school, or fishing next to a cool stream; or a cool day on the golf course.

Peace in our circumstances, like having your bills all paid; or all your deadlines are met; or no job pressures. A night at home when no one else is there; or you're in good health.

These things are good and certainly can make life a little better. But there is only one source of True Peace – Jehovah Shalom – The Lord is Peace.

Galatians 5:22 includes Peace as one of the Fruit of the Spirit. Isaiah 9:6 says Jesus is the Prince of Peace: *"For unto us a child is born, unto us a son is given, and the government will be on his shoulders. And he will be called Wonderful, Counselor, Mighty God, Everlasting Father, and Prince of Peace."*

In John 14:27 Jesus said: *"Peace I leave with you, my peace I give you. I do not give to you as the world gives, do not let your hearts be troubled and do not be afraid."* Year by year the complexities of this world grow more and more troubled and so each year we need all the more to seek peace and comfort in joyful simplicities.

It is obvious that grace and peace are the common denominations in all of these verses. Peace is to be evident in our lives. It is the Peace of God that transcends all understanding. This is what Paul was talking about in Philippians 4:4-7:

"Rejoice in the Lord always. Again, I say rejoice. Let your gentleness be evident to all. The Lord is near. Do not be anxious about anything, but in everything by prayer and petition with thanksgiving, present your request to God. And the Peace of God which transcends all understanding will guard your hearts and your minds in Christ Jesus."

Thessalonians 2:16 says: *"Now may the Lord of Peace himself give you peace at all times and in every way. The Lord be with all of you."* According to this verse, the source of Peace is the Lord. Peace has nothing at all to do with our circumstances, but everything to do with knowing who God is.

Why do you suppose Peace requires such an effort to obtain? According to Jesus in John 16:33 it says: "I have told you these things so that in me you may have Peace. In this world you will have troubles, but take heart. I have overcome the world even as you will overcome." Sometimes we forget about the Peace we have in God because we get so distracted by the troubles of this world. It all depends on where we put our focus on – the problem(s) or on God.

Isaiah 57:21 says, *"There is no Peace for the wicked."* So where do you suppose the wicked who have NO peace? They are amongst us here on earth. We were all born into a sin nature. Consequently, just as the result of one trespass was condemnation for all men, so also the result of one act of righteousness was justification that brings life for all men. *"For just as through the disobedience of one man, many were made sinners, so also through the obedience of the one man, many will be made righteous."*

How do we find Peace?

Romans 5: 1-2: *"Therefore, since we have been justified through faith, we have Peace with God through our Lord Jesus Christ, through whom we have gained access by faith into this grace in which we now stand."*

Romans 8: 6-7: *"The mind of sinful man is death, but the mind controlled by the Spirit is life and Peace; the sinful mind is hostile to God. It does not submit to God's law, nor can it do so."*

Galatians 5:25: *"Since we live by the Spirit, let us keep in step with the Spirit." So, we choose daily to crucify the flesh with its passions and desires and we choose God's way. We walk by the Spirit, we set our minds on the Spirit."*

Isaiah 26:3 - *"You will keep in perfect peace him whose mind is steadfast, because he trusts in you."*

Romans 8:28: *"And we know that in all things God works for the good of those who love him, who have been called according to his purpose."* And, I Peter 5:7: *"Cast all your anxiety on him because he cares for you."*

You see, God's mercies are new every morning. He knows your heart and he knows your needs. Take courage, no matter what circumstances surround you, no matter what your status in life, no matter what type of troubles you face, the Peace of God that passeth all understanding is there for you too.

Look again at Philippians 4:7 - "*And the peace of God, which transcends all understanding, will guard your hearts and your minds in Christ Jesus.*" John 16:33 - "*I have told you these things, so that in me you may have peace. In this world you will have trouble. But take heart! I have overcome the world.*"

When we come to Him in prayer with thanksgiving, he promises Peace that surpasses all understanding. We must choose to accept that promise and take God at His Word. We must appropriate that Peace in our lives. In other words, we must examine our life to see what is causing us anxiety or worry or loss of contentment. In every circumstance, every situation you can choose panic, chaos, worry, speculation or you can choose Peace that comes from God.

Whenever you identify an area in your life that is causing anxiety or worry, confess it to God in prayer and then apply God's peace to that specific area in your life.

So, be sure to grab a cart full of the Peace of God, which transcends all of our understanding.

PART TWO

This second group – beginning with **patience, kindness, and goodness** – contains social virtues relating to our thoughts and actions towards our fellow man and our attitude during trials and tribulations.

CHAPTER 4
GATHER UP A TON OF PATIENCE (LONG-SUFFERING)

Galatians 5: 22-23
(But the fruit of the Spirit is love, joy, peace, PATIENCE, kindness, goodness, faithfulness, gentleness, self-control; against such things there is no law.)

The Greek definition for Patience is Makrothumia, which means to endure, forbearance, soft, fortitude and temper.

There's an old African Proverb that reads: "There is Value in the Valley." The 23rd Psalms says, *"Tho I walk through the valley of the shadow of death, I will fear no evil..."* Why, because thou art with me, the Lord said.

The quality of patience evokes images of stoicism, tolerance and passivity in most people's mind. Though some of these elements are contained within the scope of what the Bible reveals of this very important Fruit of the Spirit, it is far too rich in meaning to be limited to one.

We all know people who are easily irritated. They invariably let others know it, either by a steady stream of grumbling, carping and griping accompanied by a face torn with the pain of having to suffer the fools surrounding them, or they "blow up" in red-faced fury, shouting a torrent of invective intended to let everyone within hearing distance know they have been put upon and have "had it." Some of us may not show much agitation on the outside, but inwardly we are churning with varying degrees of stress, wishing that people would "just get on with it" so we can do our thing.

The two hardest tests to master are the patience to wait for the right moment and the courage not to react or be disappointed with what we encounter.

Patience is not the ability to wait. Patience is to be calm no matter what happens, constantly take action to turn it to positive growth opportunities, and have faith to believe that it will all work out in the end "**while you are waiting.**"

Patience According to Wikipedia
Patience or forbearance is the state of endurance under difficult circumstances such as: perseverance and/or the ability to wait in the face of delay; provocation without responding in negative annoyance/anger, or exhibiting forbearance when under strain, especially when faced with longer-term difficulties. Patience is the level of endurance one can have before they allow negativity in. It is also used to refer to the character trait of being steadfast.

Definition of Patience according to a young student:
The ability to remain calm when dealing with a difficult or annoying situation, task, or person. Synonyms of Patience include: forbearance, long-suffering sufferance, tolerance.

Words related to Patience:
resignation
passiveness, passivity
amenability, compliance, conformism, docility, obedience, subordination, tractability, willingness
discipline, self-control
submission, submissiveness, defiance
contrariness, disobedience, insubordination, intractability, recalcitrance, resistance, willfulness, impatience

"No pain that we suffer, no trial that we experience is wasted. It ministers to our education, to the development of such qualities as PATIENCE; faith, fortitude and humility. All that we suffer and all that we endure, especially when we endure it patiently, builds up our characters, purifies our hearts, expands our souls, and makes us more tender and charitable, more worthy to be called the children of God; and it is through sorrow and suffering, toil and tribulation, that we gain the education that we come here to acquire and which will make none of us ever come close to exhibiting patience like our God.

Although one could not say we persecute Him as men persecute each other, yet in our own way we do bring a form of persecution on Him by our attitudes and our way of life. We often live without care for His feelings about us and His creation, behaving as much as the world does, as though neither He nor His law exists

The Bible reveals God's patience as a quality of His character that deters Him for long periods from retaliating against those who sin against Him. This fits neatly with what Peter says regarding Christ's example:

Who, when He was reviled, did not revile in return; when He suffered, He did not threaten, but committed Himself to Him who judges righteously. (I Peter 2:23).

As a man, Christ did not strike back, but wisely and patiently left any retaliation due in the matter to God's judgment.

So, be sure to grab a ton of patience and turn a negative situation into a positive growth opportunity.

Patience

Fruit of the Spirit

CHAPTER 5
YOU WILL NEED LOTS OF
KINDNESS

Galatians 5: 22-23
(But the fruit of the Spirit is love, joy, peace, patience,
KINDNESS*, goodness, faithfulness, gentleness, self-control;*
against such things there is no law.)

Kindness looks just like Goodness – they are actually Siamese twins

The Greek word for Kindness is Chrestotes, or usefulness, goodness, gentleness, gracious and kind.

This study is about kindness and goodness at the same time. They are mirrors of each other. When you see one, you most likely will see the other close by.

So, what does it mean to be Kind?

It has been stated by many that kindness is the sincere desire for the happiness of others. Goodness is the activity calculated to advance that happiness. Kindness is thinking of others. Goodness is the doing. If kindness is the **thinking,** then goodness is the **doing**.

Although you may think that kindness and goodness are the exact same thing. They are not, but they are close. Let's look at the following definitions to see if we can distinguish the difference between kindness and goodness:

Acts 10, verse 37-38 - *"You know what has happened throughout Judea, beginning in Galilee after the baptism that John preached- how God anointed Jesus of Nazareth with the Holy Spirit and power, and how he went around doing good and healing all who were under the power of the devil, because God was with him."*

The word healing in this context doesn't limit itself to just physical healing; it can be mental, emotional or spiritual healing as well. Jesus of Nazareth was anointed with the Holy Spirit, and with power. Jesus went about doing good, healing the whole body; all who were oppressed by the devil, for God was with Him. Jesus went about meeting the needs of other people, showing kindness and goodness.

A lot of times we exhibit kindness when we think about other people, desiring good things or happiness for others. **Kindness is just the beginning. It is like a seed that God plants in our lives through the Holy Spirit. Goodness is the next step** that God wants us to take through the power and guidance of the Holy Spirit. It may be helping someone by providing food or shelter or clothing. It could be that we might be called upon to provide transportation for the elderly or sick. Or maybe God will lead you to visit the sick and those that are unable to leave their homes due to age or disabilities. It certainly involves witnessing to unbelievers. There are lots of other ways not listed above that we can extend goodness to others.

Jesus demonstrated acts of Kindness for us:

Mathew 8: 1-3: When he came down from the mountainside, large crowds followed him. A man with leprosy came and knelt before him and said, *"Lord, if you are willing, you can make me clean."* Jesus reached out his hand and touched the man. *"I am willing,"* he said. *"Be clean!"* Immediately he was cured of his leprosy.' **Jesus expressed kindness** when he reached out his hand and said to the man *"I am willing"*. Jesus was sympathetic to the man's condition.

Jesus saw the man's faith. Leprosy was a dreaded disease and lepers were avoided and shunned. By reaching out His hand and touching the man, Jesus was demonstrating kindness. Jesus didn't stop there, **He showed forth goodness** by performing a miracle when He said to the man *"Be clean!"* and the man was cured of his leprosy.

Mathew 14: 13-21: When Jesus heard what had happened, he withdrew by boat privately to a solitary place. Hearing of this, the crowds followed him on foot from the towns. When Jesus landed and saw a large crowd, he had compassion on them and healed the sick. As evening approached, the disciples came to him and said, *"This is a remote place, and it's already getting late. Send the crowds away, so they can go to the villages and buy themselves some food."* Jesus replied, *"They do not need to go away. You give them something to eat."*

But the disciples said, *"We have here only five loaves of bread and two fish,"* they answered. *"Bring them here to me,"* Jesus said. And he directed the people to sit down on the grass. Taking the five loaves and the two fish and looking up to heaven, he gave thanks and broke the loaves. Then he gave them to the disciples, and the disciples gave them to the people. They all ate and were satisfied, and the disciples picked up twelve basketfuls of broken pieces that were left over. The number of those who ate was about five thousand men, besides women and children.' In these verses we see **acts of kindness and acts of goodness**.

Just prior to this event, Jesus had heard that John the Baptist had been beheaded. Herod the king had given the order for John's beheading. Jesus was needing some time alone and had withdrawn to a solitary place. The crowds probably did not know that Jesus wanted some time alone; they just wanted to be near him so they followed him. Jesus didn't tell them to go away because he needed some time alone, rather he **demonstrated kindness** to them by having compassion on them. He then **demonstrated goodness** by healing their sick. As the day progressed, the disciples suggested that Jesus send the crowds away so that they could go to their villages and buy themselves some food. This may have been a kind gesture on the part of the disciples as they were some distance away from the nearest village.

When the kindness and the love of God our Savior appeared, he saved us, not because of righteous things we had done, but because of his mercy. He saved us through the washing of rebirth and renewal by the Holy Spirit, whom he poured out on us generously through Jesus Christ our Savior, so that, having been justified by his grace, we might become heirs having the hope of eternal life." Verse 3 describes the lost condition we are in before salvation. See verse 4 and 5 which states, *"But when the kindness and love of God our Savior appeared, he saved us..."*

When the kindness of God our Savior and His love for mankind appeared, it doesn't stop there. The next verse, the next three words are the goodness. That's the goodness that God showed to us. That Christ followed through by dying on the cross for us to take our place so that we could be justified and become joint heirs with Christ and have the hope of eternal life. That is the doing on the part of Christ. He saved us. He went to the cross. **That was the goodness that he showed us.**

In Galatians 5:13: "*You, my brothers, were called to be free. But do not use your freedom to indulge the sinful nature; rather, serve one another in love.*" Ephesians 4:32: *"**Be kind** and compassionate to one another, forgiving each other, just as in Christ God forgave you.*" Ephesians 5:1-2: "*Be imitators of God, therefore, as dearly loved children and live a life of love, just as Christ loved us and gave himself up for us as a fragrant offering and sacrifice to God.*"

"**Acts of Kindness**" almost always are precursors to "**Acts of Goodness**". Be sensitive to the leading of the Holy Spirit when He is urging you to show acts of kindness. And remember not to quench the leading of the Holy Spirit by failing to see the opportunity provided for the acts of goodness that God wants to provide through you to touch the lives of others.

So, be sure to grab lots of kindness and imitate Jesus by helping others and doing good.

CHAPTER 6
PICK UP A BASKET OF
GOODNESS

Galatians 5: 22-23
(But the fruit of the Spirit is love, joy, peace, patience, kindness, GOODNESS, faithfulness, gentleness, self-control; against such things there is no law.)

Goodness looks just like Kindness – they are actually Siamese twins.

The Greek word for Goodness is Ibchah, which means to turn, to be gentle, gracious and kind.

Ephesians 4:32: *"Be kind and compassionate to one another, forgiving each other, just as in Christ God forgave you."* Ephesians 5:1-2: *"Be imitators of God, therefore, as dearly loved children and live a life of love, just as Christ loved us and gave himself up for us as a fragrant offering and sacrifice to God."*

Acts 10: 37-38: *"You know what has happened throughout Judea, beginning in Galilee after the baptism that John preached-how God anointed Jesus of Nazareth with the Holy Spirit and power, and how he went around doing good and healing all who were under the power of the devil, because God was with him."*

Jesus went about doing good, healing the whole body, all who were oppressed by the devil, for God was with Him. Jesus went about meeting the needs of other people, showing kindness and goodness.

A lot of times we exhibit goodness when we think about other people, desiring good things or happiness for others. In other words, will I calculate the activity that is necessary to advance goodness in some way?" **Goodness** is just the beginning. It is like a seed that God plants in our lives through the Holy Spirit.

Goodness is what God wants us to take through the power and guidance of the Holy Spirit. It may be helping someone by providing food or shelter or clothing. It could be that we might be called upon to provide transportation for the elderly or sick. Or maybe God will lead you to visit the sick and those that are unable to leave their homes due to age or disabilities. It certainly involves witnessing to unbelievers. There are lots of other ways not listed that we can extend goodness to others.

'Now he had to go thru Samaria. So, he came to a town in Samaria, near the plot of ground Jacob had given to his son Joseph. "Sir," the woman said, "you have nothing to draw with and the well is deep. Where can you get this living water? Are you greater than our father Jacob, who gave us the well and drank from it himself, as did also his sons and his flocks and herds?" Jesus answered, "Everyone who drinks this water will be thirsty again, but whoever drinks the water I give him will never thirst. Indeed, the water I give him will become in him a spring of water welling up to eternal life." The woman said to him, "Sir, give me this water so that I won't get thirsty and have to keep coming here to draw water." He told her, "Go, call your husband and come back."

"I have no husband," she replied. Jesus said to her, *"You are right when you say you have no husband. The fact is, you have had five husbands, and the man you now have is not your husband. What you have just said is quite true."* "Sir," the woman said, *"I can see that you are a prophet. Our fathers worshiped on this mountain, but you Jews claim that the place where we must worship is in Jerusalem."* Jesus declared, *"Believe me, woman, a time is coming when you will* worship the Father neither on this mountain nor in Jerusalem. You Samaritans worship what you do not know; we worship what we do know, for salvation is from the Jews. Yet a time is coming and has now come when the true worshipers will worship the Father in spirit and truth, for they are the kind of worshipers the Father seeks. God is spirit, and his worshipers must worship in spirit and in truth."

The woman said, "I know that Messiah (called Christ) is coming. When he comes, he will explain everything to us." Then Jesus declared, "I who speak to you am he." Just then his disciples returned and were surprised to find him talking with a woman. But no one asked, "What do you want?" or "Why are you talking with her?" Then, leaving her water jar, the woman went back to the town and said to the people, "Come, see a man who told me everything I ever did. Could this be the Christ?" They came out of the town and made their way toward him. Many of the Samaritans from that town believed in him because of the woman's testimony, **"He told me everything I ever did."**

We see in these verses a miracle being performed. We now see goodness in action. How many times do we do well when it comes to acts of kindness but fail to follow through with acts of goodness? It's important not only to be sympathetic and compassionate to others (**acts of kindness**), we should also follow through by actually helping others (**acts of goodness**). And as illustrated in the verses above, it's not important how much or how little we have, what's important is that we are willing to follow the leadership of the **Holy Spirit to touch lives through both Acts of Kindness and Acts of Goodness.**

So, pick up a basket full of goodness by doing good for others and going about healing the sick.

Goodness
Galatians 5:22-25

Fruit of the Spirit

PART THREE

*This third group beginning with – **faithfulness, gentleness, and self-control** – which deals with those attributes that are disciplined, orderly, and have a productive life; and provides principles for the believer's proper conduct towards others.*

CHAPTER 7
DON'T FORGET A BIG SACK OF FAITHFULNESS

Galatians 5: 22-23
(But the fruit of the Spirit is love, joy, peace, patience, kindness, goodness, FAITHFULNESS, gentleness, self-control; against such things there is no law.)

The Greek word for Faithfulness is Mahahh, which means to hesitate, to be reluctant, to delay, to depend on, to linger, or to tarry.

God's faithfulness is proclaimed throughout the entire book of Psalms. Just one example is Psalms chapter 117 - "Praise the LORD, all you nations, extol him, all you peoples. For great is his love toward us, and the faithfulness of the LORD endures forever. Praise the LORD."

Faithfulness hinges upon what we value as important combined with commitment. Humans have a powerful tendency to be faithful to what they think is truly important, be it a family name, spouse, friendship, employer, school, athletic team or even certain things like a make of automobile.

This tendency was an issue when the disciples decided to follow Peter's lead and return to their fishing trade after Jesus' death and resurrection. In John 21: 15-17, Jesus pointedly asks Peter three times whether he loved Him. The first time He asks whether he loved Him "more than these," referring either to his fellow apostles or the tools of his fishing trade. The inference is inescapable: Jesus wanted Peter to hold Him of greater importance than anything on earth. Considering Peter's weighty responsibility, he could not be faithful to Jesus without the staunchest commitment to Him as most important of all in his life.

The meaning to us is clear here. We must love Christ supremely, or we do not love Him much at all. If we are not willing to give up all earthly possessions, forsake all earthly friends, and obey Him above all others, including our own carnal desires to be faithful to Him, our attachment to Him is ingenious at best. Is such a proposition too much? Does not marriage require a similar faithfulness from each spouse? Without it, it is no wonder there is so much adultery and divorce in the church.

Holding true to the course God has laid before us is difficult amid this world's many alluring distractions clamoring for our time and attention. This world is attractive to human nature and temp us to expend our energies in self-satisfaction. Jesus warns all who take up their cross that the way is difficult and narrow, requiring a great deal of vision and discipline to be faithful to His cause. Some have completed the course. Those who held God and His way in the highest esteem in their lives are awaiting those of us traveling the path now.

What Does Faithfulness Mean?

"Faithfulness" does not even appear in the New Testament of the King James version (KJV). However, the idea certainly does in the Greek. In the listing of the Fruit of the Spirit in Galatians 5: 22, modern translation renders the word that the KJV translates into "faith" as "faithfulness."

It means "good faith, sincerity;" being faithful, sincere. The English usage of being "faithful" defines *faithful* as "maintaining allegiance, constant, loyal, marked by or showing a strong sense of duty or responsibility, conscientious, accurate, reliable, and exact."

Webster Dictionary compares "faithful" with its synonyms: *Faithful* implies steadfast adherence to a person or thing to which one is bound as by an oath or obligation; *loyalty* implies undeviating allegiance to a person, cause, institution, etc. which one feels morally bound to support or defend; *constant* suggests freedom from fickleness in affections or loyalties; or a strong allegiance to one's principles or purposes as not to be turned aside by any cause; *resolute* stresses unwavering determination, often in adhering to one's personal ends or aims. Other synonyms include dedicated, steadfast, devoted, dependable, accurate, true, conscientious, dutiful, careful, scrupulous and thorough.

The opposite of Faithfulness is Faithlessness which means not keeping faith; dishonest; disloyal; unreliable; undependable; unbelieving. Its synonyms include doubting, treacherous and unscrupulous.

Faithlessness in the End Time

The apostle Paul writes in II Timothy 3:13; that *"evil men (and impostors) will grow worse and worse, deceiving and being deceived."* People today are no different from when Paul his epistles, but the occasion to sin, the incentive to do so and thus sin's frequency and intensity are at their highest levels since just before the Flood. In other words, the environment to commit sin more easily grows ever more amenable, and human nature is taking advantage of it. We have been born into—indeed have unwittingly contributed to creating an environment in which it is exceedingly difficult to remain faithful.

We live in a world in which self-centeredness is being promoted to its greatest extent in human history. Appealing advertising hammers away at us to gratify ourselves: Why wait, why deny ourselves, why sacrifice, why not go along with everyone else?

Constantly we hear, "Indulge yourself because you deserve it." This world always appeals to moral and ethical standards lower than those of the great God and His way of life. In Technicolor with emotion-stirring music, Hollywood "sells" adultery and fornication as acceptable as long as the couple involved are attractive and somehow oppressed—thus "deserving" of a "better" relationship.

War, murder, lying, stealing, coveting, Sabbath-breaking and idolatry are acts that almost everyone in the world would claim as being wrong, yet most unwittingly commit them to some degree and promote them in our culture. They justify their sin because everybody else is doing it, and they see no good reason why they should not just go along. If they try to swim against the tide, they think they will be taken advantage of.

Not too long ago, a person's word was his bond, and mere handshakes sealed major business agreements. Faithlessness is playing a major role in this destruction. People are without natural affection and traitors to their marital contract. Child abuse is becoming ever more prevalent. Athletes seem to break contracts almost at will. Manufacturers lie about the quality of their products, and workers fudge in the quality of their work.

Faithlessness is rising to its peak because self-centeredness, the father of irresponsibility, is being promoted to its utmost. It is the spirit of this age, but we have cause to resist it by what God has offered us in His revelation. God-centeredness in our lives is the answer to faithlessness and irresponsibility. But God-centeredness is not cheap, and few are willing to pay the price: their lives!

An Overview of God's Faithfulness

As with all the Fruit of the Spirit, God Himself is the model we must study for examples of faithfulness to encourage us to trust and to emulate Him. The faithfulness of God is a familiar phrase to those of a religious mind, but its depth and scope are probably not as familiar. God's faithfulness seems to have been a favorite subject of Paul's. He writes of it in his first epistle (I Thessalonians) and again in what may have been his last (II Timothy). Paul had proved it in a thousand dangers and struggles; he found that, when all was said and done, God had never failed him.

When we speak of one another as faithful, we mean that we adhere to our word, that we keep faith with men and that we discharge the obligations of our office or position. Because of these things, we are trustworthy. It is much the same when we think and speak of God's faithfulness.

Usually, the first idea that comes to mind when God is called faithful is that He keeps His promises. This, of course, is included in the concept of God's faithfulness, but it is interesting that it appears only twice in the New Testament.

II Timothy 2:23 this verse tells us that we can trust Him all the way to death because "*He cannot deny Himself.*" God's very nature and character constitute a solemn obligation that He is His own law, that He is bound by what He is and that He can never be even in the smallest degree contradictory to or less than the level of His own consistent and uniform self.

"*For the flesh lusts against the Spirit, and the Spirit against the flesh.*" Galatians 5:17; and we frequently lose the battle because the divine nature does not completely fill our minds. We grow hot and cold and drop below our best selves.

No man is always himself, but God is always Himself! With God it is as the apostle John says, "*God is light and in Him is no darkness at all*" There is nothing in God that opposes His faithfulness in carrying out His Word. Our calling to Christ is one of God's past acts. This means that what God has begun in us He will complete all the way to salvation

God's Faithfulness and Trials

With the understanding of God's faithfulness, we can apply this principle to other areas of our Christian life that are of practical and daily importance. By this we can be assured that He will deal with us in a patient, merciful, generous and yet persistent manner.

Very early in the Bible gives us examples of God's faithfulness that helped to perfect those undergoing trials: "Then God remembered Noah, and every living thing, and all the animals that were with him in the ark. And God made a wind to pass over the earth and the waters subsided" Genesis 8:1; It is good to first consider that God's faithfulness covers animal life as well as human life. He upholds "all things by the word of His power." He does not simply create and then leave His creations to their own devices. His obligation to all life and its care and sustenance continues unabated.

Though the words of this verse are few and simple, to those who feel lost in the depth of an ongoing trial a world of meaning lies here: We are not lost to God. Noah, his family and animals were virtually imprisoned in the ark for months, pitching about alone on an endless sea. Nothing broke the skyline. Noah could have easily thought himself as forgotten. Though he could remind himself that God had promised him protection, where was God now—now when the gray days and black nights dragged by and wherever he looked he saw only empty waters and a sky that seemed to hold no hope?

We may never have to face a trial of the magnitude that Noah faced, but God's faithfulness promises another great assurance: It guarantees that all our trials will be in proportion to our strength. God pledges through Paul in I Corinthians 10:13; *"No temptation has overtaken you except such as is common to man; but God is*

FAITHFUL, who will not allow you to be tempted beyond what you are able, but with the temptation will also make the way of escape, that you may be able to bear it."*

God will never lay on us anything beyond our power to overcome. He knows how much pressure our hearts can stand. Do teachers give college-level assignments to a first grader and expect them to perform? No. Men are careful not to overload a truck, horse, mule or ox. Will God be any less merciful and faithful to us, His children He is creating in His image? He clearly recognizes His obligation to the work of His own hands to supply our needs and shape the burdens needed to prepare us for His Kingdom.

God's Faithfulness and Forgiveness

Earlier, we saw that one of God's past acts was calling us to be in Christ. Paul confirms this as an act of God's faithfulness. *"God is faithful, by whom you were called into the fellowship of His Son, Jesus Christ our Lord."* Our calling would go nowhere beyond a meaningless invitation if God was not faithful to forgive our sins. Without forgiveness and cleansing, there is no access to Him, and thus no relationship with Him blossoms and grows.

"Therefore, having been justified by faith, we have peace with God through our Lord Jesus Christ, through whom also we have access by faith into this grace in which we stand, and rejoice in hope of the glory of God."

One can justifiably say that this expression of God's faithfulness is the pivot upon which turns His whole purpose for humanity. God calls and then through His goodness leads us to repentance (Romans 10:9-10) adds, *"If we confess our sins, He is faithful and just to forgive us our sins and to cleanse us from all unrighteousness."*

Since Christ has come and died that we might be pardoned and cleansed, God's faithfulness is part of His grace. He would not be faithful to His promises, His past acts in Christ's works, or His calling that has sounded in our ears unless, when we obeyed the call and confessed, He allowed us to enter into the full possession of His pardoning grace. In other words, our forgiveness and cleansing, the receiving of favor from Him, is a product of His faithfulness.

God's faithfulness in these areas has far-reaching, practical ramifications for us. That God is faithful means that His character is unchangingly consistent. The unalterable structure of the universe consists of both justice and forgiveness. God never acts in contradiction of Himself, and in all experiences, we may depend on Him to be unalterably just and forgiving toward us. **Because He is faithful, He can be the central and most important object of our faith**. Could we trust a god if we were never sure what he might do?

What Is Our Responsibility?

This day the Lord your God commands you to observe these statutes and judgments; therefore, you shall be careful to observe them with all your heart and with all your soul. Today you have proclaimed the Lord to be your God, and that you will walk in His ways and keep His statues, His commandments, and His judgments, and that you will obey His voice. Also, today the Lord has proclaimed you to be His special people, just as He has promised you, that you should keep all His commandments, and that He will set you high above all nations which He has made, in praise, in name, and in honor, and that you may be a holy people to the Lord your God, just as He has spoken.

Since God is faithful, it has become our responsibility to imitate Him in being faithful by committing our lives to well doing. In II Corinthians 1:17-19, Paul demonstrates from his own life what this means. *"Therefore, when I was planning this, did I do it lightly? Or *the things I plan, do I plan according to the flesh, that with me, there should be Yes, Yes, and No, No? But as God is faithful, our word to you was not Yes and No. For the Son of God, Jesus Christ, who was preached among you by us—by me, Silvanus, and Timothy—was not Yes and No, but in Him was Yes."*

Because God is faithful, the strength to be faithful is promised to us in Hebrews 4:16 assures us, *"Let us therefore come boldly to the throne of grace, that we may obtain mercy and find grace to help in time of need."* Forgiveness, access to His throne, and the promises of His Spirit and that no trial will be greater than we can bear, combined with His declaration that He works in us both to will and to do, assure us that this fruit of the Spirit can be produced in us when we yield as faithful servants.

So, be sure to grab a sack full of faithfulness and allow God's Spirit to move into all areas of your life so that faithfulness becomes a way of life for you. People around you will then be able to see the love of God through your faithful living.

THE FRUIT OF THE SPIRIT IS

FAITHFULNESS

Lesson 8

CHAPTER 8
GRAB TWO HANDFULLS OF
GENTLENESS

Galatians 5: 22-23
(But the fruit of the Spirit is love, joy, peace, patience, kindness, goodness, faithfulness, GENTLENESS, self-control; against such things there is no law.)

The Greek word for Gentleness is Cillown, which means to forgive, to pardon, or to spare.

Gentleness has been defined in the following ways: Mildness in dealing with others. Gentleness displays a sensitive regard for others and is careful never to be unfeeling for the rights of others.

Gentleness is an active trait describing the manner in which we should treat others. It is the grace which pervades the whole nature, mellowing all which would be harsh. Likened to the harmlessness of a dove. Gentleness distinguishes between these two "**gentleness -vs- meekness**" in the same way the Greek writers do, **gentleness** is an active trait describing the manner in which we should treat others. **Meekness** is a passive trait describing the proper Christian response when others mistreat us. Both (gentleness & meekness) are born of power, NOT weakness.

Isaiah 40: 10, *"See, the Sovereign LORD comes with power, and his arm rules for him. See, his reward is with him, and his recompense accompanies him."* Isaiah 40:15 - *"Surely the nations are like a drop in a bucket; they are regarded as dust on the scales; he weighs the islands as though they were fine dust."*

Isaiah 40: 25-26, *"To whom will you compare me? Or who is my equal?" says the Holy One. Lift up your eyes and look to the heavens: Who created all these? He who brings out the starry host one by one, and calls them each by name. Because of his great power and mighty strength, not one of them is missing.'*

Isaiah 40:11 - He tends his flock like a shepherd: He gathers the lambs in his arms and carries them close to his heart; he **gently** leads those that have young. In the midst of this power is gentleness. We should never confuse gentleness with weakness.

Gentleness is the way we treat others - The gentleness of Christ is described in Mathew 11: 28-30, *"Come to me, all you who are weary and burdened, and I will give you rest.... For my yoke is easy and my burden is light."* What better time to receive the gentleness of Christ than when we are burdened, heavy laden, weighted down by life's pressures (demands of family, job pressures, finances, not enough time in the day, etc.)

Does the word "rest" in the preceding verse mean to lay down and stop working or giving up on everything? No. Rest is not inactivity; "rest" is an inward tranquility while one performs necessary labor. The Lord promises inner tranquility to the weary and heavy laden who come to Him while they are engaged in our daily yet necessary labor.

"Meekness - refers to the passive way we respond to others when we are mistreated" - Meekness is not occupied with self, what belongs to it, what is right by it or how it should be treated. According to Vines Expository Dictionary, it is an inwrought grace of the soul; and the exercise of it is first and chiefly love towards God. It is that temper of the spirit in which we accept

His dealings with us as good, and therefore without disputing or resisting; it is only the humble heart which is also the meek, and which, as such, does not fight against God and more or less struggle and contend with Him.

Vines Expository Dictionary also states It must be clearly understood, therefore, that the meekness manifested by the Lord and commended to the believer is the **Fruit Under Power**.

The common assumption is that when a man is meek it is because he cannot help himself; but the Lord was 'meek' because He had the infinite resources of God at His command. Meekness does not denote an outward expression of feelings but an inward grace of the soul, calmness toward God. It is accepting God's dealing with us, considering them as good in that they enhance the closeness of our relationship with Him. Meekness does not blame God for the persecutions and evil doings of men.

The greatest examples of meekness were seen in the last hours of Jesus' life before He died on the cross. Let's look at these:

Triumphal Entry into Jerusalem

Jesus rides into Jerusalem on a young donkey. *'Jesus found a young donkey and sat upon it, as it is written, "Do not be afraid, O Daughter of Zion; see, your king is coming, seated on a donkey's colt."'* (John Chapter 12: 14-15) You might be wondering, what does the fact that Jesus rode into Jerusalem on a donkey have to do with meekness. For that answer we need to look in the Old Testament

"Rejoice greatly, O Daughter of Zion! Shout, Daughter of Jerusalem! See, your king comes to you, righteous and having salvation, gentle and riding on a donkey, on a colt, the foal of a donkey." (Zechariah 9: 9) This verse found in the Old Testament describes how the Messiah will enter into Jerusalem and also specifically states that He is gentle. Jesus did not enter Jerusalem riding on a mighty stallion; rather He chose to enter Jerusalem riding on a young donkey. The symbolism is clear, **riding on a young donkey symbolized gentleness and meekness.**

Consider the two thieves that were crucified on either side of Jesus. One thief was casting insults at Jesus. Look at the dialogue that took place between the other thief and Jesus: 'Then he said, "Jesus, remember me when you come into your kingdom." Jesus answered him, *"I tell you the truth, today you will be with me in paradise."* (Luke 23: 22-43). Even while nailed to the cross, Jesus responds with gentleness and a promise. Jesus willingly laid down His life for others, the ultimate sacrifice.

Remember, He could have called down over 72,000 angels to destroy the entire world if He so chose. But He chose to stay on the cross, to die for our sins, for our good, so that we could be saved. Jesus had a humble heart; He was committed to doing the Father's will. By dying on the cross, accepting upon Himself the punishment that we deserved, He accomplished the Father's will and glorified God the Father.

"So, whether you eat or drink or whatever you do, do it all for the glory of God. Do not cause anyone to stumble, whether Jews, Greeks or the church of God-- even as I try to please everybody in every way. For I am not seeking my own good but the good of many, so that they may be saved. Follow my example, as I follow the example of Christ." (I Corinthians 10: 31; and 11: 1) *"Whatever you do, do all to the glory of God."*

So, be sure to grab two handfuls of gentleness, and when we treat others with gentleness, we glorify the Father. When we respond in meekness to the mistreatment directed toward us by others, we glorify the Father.

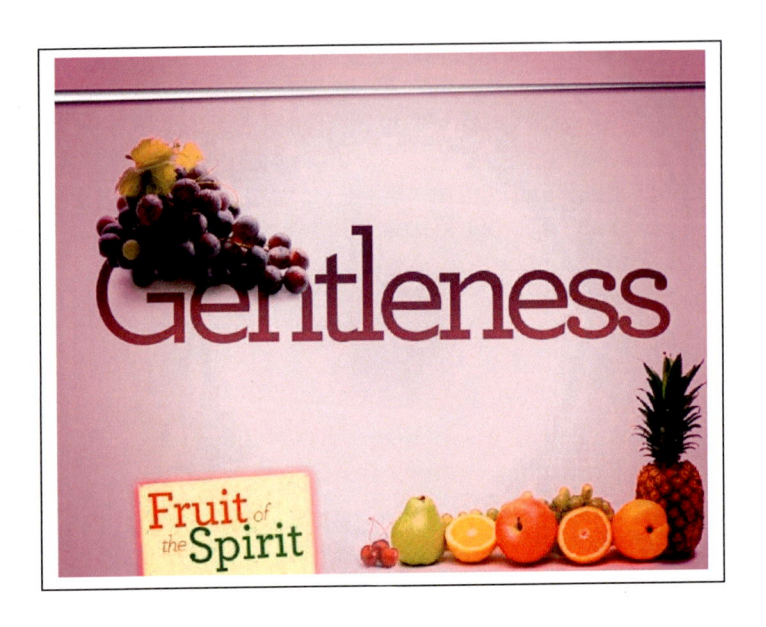

Gentleness

Fruit of the Spirit

CHAPTER 9
FILL YOUR CART FULL OF
SELF-CONTROL
(OR TEMPERANCE)

Galatians 5: 22-23
*(But the fruit of the Spirit is love, joy, peace, patience, kindness, goodness, faithfulness, gentleness, **SELF-CONTROL**; against such things there is no law.)*

The Greek word for Self-Control is Egkrateia, which means to strengthen, to acknowledge, spiritual power, or to have temperance.

I Peter 2:11 says: "*Dear friends, I urge you, as aliens and strangers in the world, to abstain from sinful desires, which war against your soul.*" Paul stated in Romans 7: 22-25 "*For in my inner being I delight in God's law; but I see another law at work in the members of my body, waging war against the law of my mind and making me a prisoner of the law of sin at work within my members. What a wretched man I am! Who will rescue me from this body of death? Thanks be to God-through Jesus Christ our Lord!*"

Question: Are you serving God with your mind, your thoughts and emotions self-control consists of 1) inner strength and 2) sound judgment. The translators of the NIV version of the Holy Bible have used the expression self- control" to translate two different words from the original language.

The first word in Galatians 5 refers to moderation or temperance in the gratification of our desires and appetites. **Self-control has the literal meaning of inner strength**, and refers to that strength of character that enables one to control his passions and desires. Self-control denotes soundness of mind or sound judgment. The word conveys the idea of allowing sound judgment to control our desires and appetites, our thoughts, emotions and actions. Sound judgment enables us to determine what we should do and how we should respond. Inner strength provides the will to do it. Both are necessary for Spirit directed self-control.

Ultimately: Self-control is the exercise of inner strength and sound judgment under the direction of the Holy Spirit that enables us to do, think and say the things that are pleasing to God.

Self-control of your thoughts means entertaining in our minds only those thoughts that are acceptable to God. We allow in our minds what we do not allow in our actions.

Psalm 139: 1-4 - "*O LORD, you have searched me and you know me. You know when I sit and when I rise; you perceive my thoughts from afar. You discern my going out and my lying down; you are familiar with all my ways. Before a word is on my tongue you know it completely, O LORD.*" How do we know if our thoughts are acceptable?

Paul said in Philippians 4: 8 - "*Finally, brothers, whatever is true, whatever is noble, whatever is right, whatever is pure, whatever is lovely, whatever is admirable - if anything is excellent or praiseworthy - think about such things.*" If you find your mind on anything other than the above, what do you do?

Corinthians 10: 3-5 - "*For though we live in this world, we do not wage war as the world does. The weapons we fight with are not the weapons of the world. On the contrary, they have divine power to demolish strongholds. We demolish arguments and every pretension that sets itself up against the knowledge of God, and we take captive every thought to make it obedient to Christ.*"

Now, let's look first at the opposite of self-control (uncontrolled temper). Proverbs 16: 32 - *"Better a patient man than a warrior, a man who controls his temper than one who takes a city."* To have a temper that requires control is not a mark of ungodliness; to fail to control it is. **Uncontrollable temper damages the self-respect of others, creates bitterness and destroys relationships.**

In addition, we should be slow to anger when we are wronged or when we perceive that acts of wrongness are being committed by others. Take note of what the psalmist had to say about God in Psalm 86: 15 - *"But you, O Lord, are a compassionate and gracious God, slow to anger, abounding in love and faithfulness."* This verse emphasizes that God is abounding in love and faithfulness. God can be provoked to anger but it doesn't happen immediately. We should strive to be more like God, slow to anger, compassionate and gracious to others. The next time you feel your anger is being kindled against someone, try praying for that person rather than becoming angry with them.

Other un-controlled emotions like resentment, bitterness and self-pity aren't as harmful to others as they are destructive to ourselves and our relationship with God. Resentment, bitterness and self-pity build up inside our hearts and eat away at our spiritual lives like a slow cancer. All of these sinful emotions have one thing in common - a focus on self. We put our disappointments, wounded pride and shattered dreams on thrones in our hearts which then become idols. We nurture resentment and bitterness and then wallow in self-pity.

God will not fail us nor forsake us. But we choose to be defiant and think on those things which do not come in line with Philippians 4: 8 *"Finally, brothers, whatever is true, whatever is noble, whatever is right, whatever is pure, whatever is lovely, whatever is admirable - if anything is excellent or praiseworthy - think about such things."*

By failing to adhere to the principles outlined in Philippians 4: 8, it is not only destructive to ourselves but it is also destructive to our faith and dishonors God.

Self-control is key. We must strive to grow in our Faith and Godliness. Sound judgment is the beginning of self-control and sound judgment must be based on the knowledge of God's Word and His standard for our bodies, thoughts and emotions. Sound judgment enables us to make an accurate estimate of our needs in the area of self-control.

Romans 12: 3 - *"For by the grace given me I say to every one of you: Do not think of yourself more highly than you ought, but rather think of yourself with sober judgment, in accordance with the measure of faith God has given you."* The battle of our thoughts and emotions begins in our hearts and minds. We must learn to take thoughts captive and destroy speculations and every lofty thing raised up against the Knowledge of God - to the obedience of Jesus Christ.

In Conclusion – We must persevere in our battle to choose what is right, not only in actions but in thoughts and emotions. We must call upon the Spirit of God to help us in our time of need realizing that we cannot accomplish this without His help and leadership.

So, let's remember to grab a cart full of self-control and create an avenue for people to use their talents (Gifts) and abilities to be used for God's glory. Because, without no practical application for your GIFTS, there's no sense in having them. Does that make sense to you? I hope so! Remember, false comparisons create an improper imbalance in your life.

THE FRUIT OF THE SPIRIT IS

SELF-CONTROL

Lesson 10

CHAPTER 10
And Finally,
Letting God fill your empty places with His fruit

Let's look again at the Woman at the Well; - It was a daily resource she'd come to depend on. A place she went to get her needs met. But it was never enough; every day she came back for more.

Filling her jar with water, the woman looked up and heard Him ask her for a drink. Then He offered her something in return: *living water*. Unlike the water she came to get that day, He said the water He offered would satisfy her so deeply she'd never thirst again.

But she had a hard time believing His promise. *"You have nothing to draw with and the well is deep. Where can you get this living water?"* (John 4:11) She asked.

What she didn't realize was that Jesus wanted to satisfy a deeper thirst in her heart — a longing He'd created to lead her heart to Him: The One and only Source that could satisfy her soul.

All He needed to draw with was His Spirit, for it would draw her near to Him. And as far as the depth of the well, it was her heart He was looking into. She was the only one who could stop Him from reaching the parts that needed Him most.

I know that place of needing Jesus to look into my heart and show me the emptiness only He can fill.

Like the woman at the well, I've depended on other means to get my needs met. Yet when I look to them, *instead of Him*, they are never enough, or never satisfying.

I know I'm not by myself when I ask; have you looked to people: family and friends, bosses, relationships, teachers and mentors, spouse and kids for meeting your needs? I've longed for their approval and the affirmation that comes with it. But, no matter how much I do or get, it's never enough to fill me up. **And it's not supposed to be.**

Why? Because the empty places in our hearts were created to be filled by God alone. The deepest thirst of our soul can only be quenched by Him. We see this deep thirst even in King David, who had everything: the highest position, unlimited possessions, and great power, yet none of it was enough. He described himself as parched and thirsty for God:

You God, are my God, earnestly I seek you; I thirst for you, my whole being longs for you, in a dry and parched land where there is no water. (Ps. 63:1) Then David went on to describe what he experienced God's love.

I have seen you in the sanctuary and beheld your power and your glory. Because your love is better than life, my lips will glorify you. I will praise you as long as I live, and in your name, I will lift up my hands.

And the same thing happened to the woman Jesus met at the well that day. She drank deeply of His love and was filled to overflow, and we can be too. Just like the woman at the well, God put a longing in our hearts that was intended to lead us back to Him.

Remember, Only His unconditional acceptance, approval and affirmation can fill the empty places in our hearts - the deepest thirst of our souls. Until God's love and acceptance is enough, nothing else will be.

So, let us start by filling our baskets with the Fruit of the Spirit and fill up on His word as we draw close to him daily.

So, be sure to stop in at anything if you need any help shopping in our little Gift Shop. Remember, everything is always FREE.

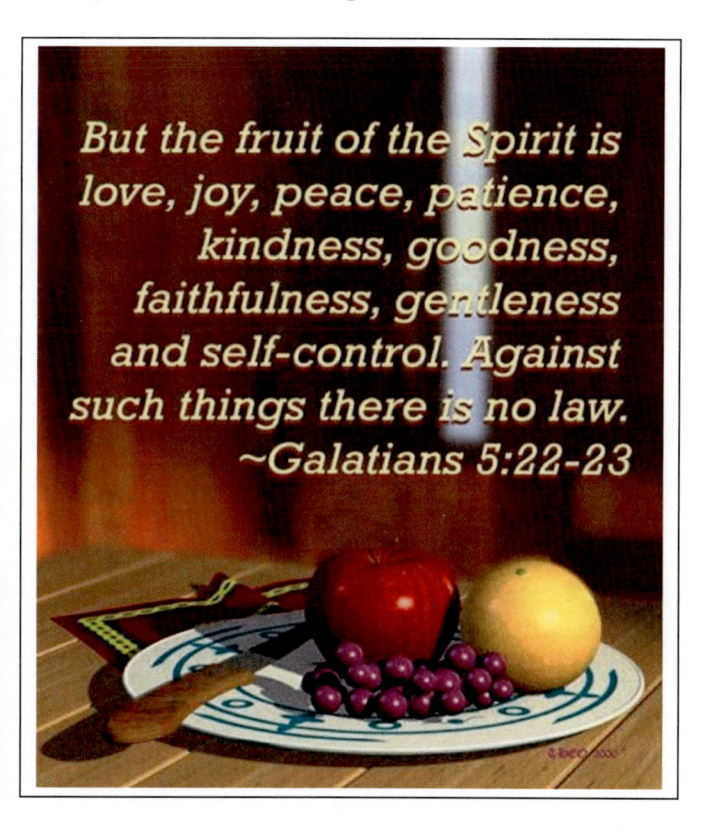

Against such things there is no law

But the fruit of the Spirit is love, joy, peace, patience, kindness, goodness, faithfulness, gentleness and self-control. Against such things there is no law.
~Galatians 5:22-23

~ TAKE A SELF INVENTORY~
HOW DO I GROW
FRUIT OF THE SPIRIT WITHIN ME?

Well, I'm glad you ask that question. Did you know having evident of the **Fruit of the Spirit** can show others that you've got Jesus in your life? Here how:

What is the fruit of the Spirit?
Galatians 5:22-23 lists nine words that describe the Fruit of the Spirit. When we have these fruit in our life, we show people we are Christians by how we act. The Fruit of the Spirit is like proof that we are becoming more and more like Jesus.

Do Christians automatically grow this fruit?
No. After we become Christians, we must choose to partner with the Holy Spirit to grow this fruit in our life. As our Bible explains, first we do our part by staying connected to Jesus, just like branches stay connected to the vine. We stay connected when we do things like praying and reading the Bible.

Does growing up help us grow the Fruit of the Spirit?
Not always. We must choose to let the Holy Spirit help us grow His fruit in our lives. Jesus doesn't expect us to grow all of the fruit at the same time. Instead, He wants us to look for His leading on which FRUIT we need to grow at that time in our lives, and then ask Him to show us how to grow. Even adults still need to choose every day to let the Fruit of the Spirit show and grow in their life. Then as we grow the fruit, we'll get better at showing others that Jesus is in our life.

Kindness
GOODNESS
FAITHFULNESS
Joy
gentleness
SELF-CONTROL
LOVE
Peace
patience

Image: Billy Alexander

fb.com/TrustHimAlways

"You God, are my God, earnestly I seek you; I thirst for you, my whole being (my mind, body, and soul) longs for you, in a dry and parched land where there is NO water." Psalm 63:1, NIV.

References:
Wikipedia
Webster Dictionary
Complete Word Study Dictionary
Webster New World Dictionary
Vines Expository Dictionary
STRONGS Exhaustive Concordance
King James Bible
NIV version of the Holy Bible
New King James Bible
Message Bible

QUESTION?

There are Nine (9) Fruit of the Spirit. Can you name them each without looking back into the chapters? Does not have to be in order.

1. _____
2. _____
3. _____
4. _____
5. _____
6. _____
7. _____
8. _____
9. _____

Which one of these above do your struggle with the most, and why?

_____
_____
_____
_____
_____
_____

You may contact the authors via email at:
brokenwingsministry@yahoo.com **or their website or on Facebook.**

Memory Scripture – Galatians 5: 22-23

The fruit of the Spirit is:
LOVE
JOY
PATIENCE
PEACE
KINDNESS
GOODNESS
FAITHFULNESS
GENTLENESS
SELF-CONTROL

Against such things there is no law.
Galatians 5:22,23

TAKE NOTES HERE

About the Authors

Elder Melvin and Jennifer Rankins, married over 40 years, they have two beautiful children, five grandchildren and one great grandson. Diversity marks the essence of their ministry, endowed with the Fruit of the Spirit and led by the Holy Spirit. They are ultimately committed to serving the Lord in ministry.

They've both successfully completed the following Certificate Programs: Marriage Works; Caring for People God's Way; Marriage Mentoring; Breaking Free, and most recently – Addiction and Recovery – a yearly requirement from the American Association of Christian Counselors in conjunction with the Center for Biblical Counseling. Currently they've completed a Certification Program in Grief Counseling.

***THE FRUIT OF THE SPIRIT
IS LIKE A BAG OF SKITTLES – ITS ALL IN THERE,
INDIVIDUALLY YET AS ONE.***

**THANK YOU FOR STOPPING IN
COME AGAIN
TO VISIT WITH US SOON**

Hope your baskets were full when you left. Feel free to stop back in The Gift Shop anytime you're getting low on any one of the nine Fruit of the Spirit.

*Remember, everything is a **FREE** Gift*

But the fruit of the Spirit is love, joy, peace, patience, kindness, goodness, faithfulness, gentleness, self-control; against such things there is no law.

Galatians 5:22-23

Please leave a review of this book on Amazon.com

thank you

ALSO BY THE AUTHORS

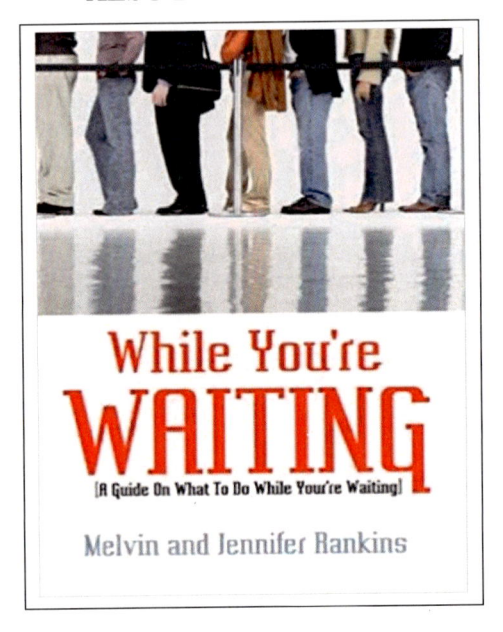

While You're Waiting
[A Guide On What To Do While You're Waiting]
Melvin and Jennifer Rankins

While You're Waiting *is a simple book that reveals profound truths that will help tens of thousands of people around the world discover the simple act of waiting. This book can be used in everyday situations and circumstances to help you do something positive while you are waiting. It would be so easy if we had an instruction manual on literally how to wait on God. But the truth is, waiting isn't easy for any of us. We hate to wait for anything, let alone waiting on God for answers to prayer. We're a microwave society where everybody wants everything now. We hope that this little book will be a blessing to all our friends, family, and colleagues because of the unique insights that make it enjoyable and a fun book for everyone who are waiting – on something.*

Made in the USA
Lexington, KY
21 February 2018